# CHILDREN of the BIBLE

**Lionel Fanthorpe**

Illustrated by
Lynette Hardwick

Patricia and I dedicate this book with all our love and gratitude to our daughters, Stephanie and Fiona, for all the joy they brought us while they were children, and all the joy which they unfailingly bring us now as adults. Only God could devise any happiness as great as that which is shared by a loving Christian family.

© 1994 Lionel Fanthorpe

**British Library Cataloguing in Publication Data**
Fanthorpe, Lionel
   Children of the Bible.
   1. Bible.
   I. Title

ISBN 1 85219 056 6

All rights reserved. No part of this publication may be reproduced, stored in a retrieval system or transmitted, in any form or by any means, electronic, mechanical, photo-copying, recording or otherwise, without prior permission of the copyright owner.

All enquiries and requests relevant to this title should be sent to the publisher, Bishopsgate Press Ltd., Bartholomew House, 15 Tonbridge Road, Hildenborough, Kent TN11 9BH
Printed in Singapore through GlobalCom Pte Ltd

# CONTENTS

Foreword by Canon Stanley Mogford, MA     4

Miriam and Baby Moses     5

Samuel Listens to God     8

David, the Brave Shepherd Boy     11

The Boy with the Arrows     14

The Poor Widow and her Son     17

The Girl who helped Captain Naaman     20

Jesus as a Boy goes to the Temple     23

The Boy who gave Jesus his Bread and Fish     26

Jesus Blesses the Children     29

St Paul is saved by his young Nephew     32

# FOREWORD

Children have begun of late to trouble the conscience of the world. Some 40,000 die every day of starvation and untreated illnesses. Allied to the plight of those little ones who die so needlessly, there is growing anxiety about the many who survive, but are so neglected or maltreated by the adults of their world some 100,000 of them, in this country alone, disappear every year from their homes.

No one, however, would be foolish enough to believe that the sufferings of children have ever been restricted to any particular age or society. Wherever there has been cruelty and disadvantage, children have always tended to bear the brunt of it.

Many such cases of child suffering are easily found in the pages of the Bible, from the infant Moses, a helpless pawn in the politics of his background, to the son of the poor widow of Zarephath whose hold on life was restricted to a handful of flour and a little cooking oil, and to the many children, in and around Bethlehem, murdered by Herod's jealous rage.

But suffering is not the whole story. In the main, children have been cherished, agonised over, fought and died for. For the normal loving adult the words of Jesus are engraved on the heart: "Suffer the little children to come unto me: For of such is the Kingdom of Heaven."

The writer of this book is just such an adult. He has children of his own whom he loves. He has spent years of his life teaching other people's children, the most loving and the most difficult among them, and has taken infinite pains over it. He now writes for them, as he once taught, in affection. Any parent and any child will be the better for having shared these Bible stories with him.

**Canon S.H. Mogford**

# MIRIAM AND BABY MOSES

Moses was born at a time when life was very hard and difficult for his people, the Hebrews. They lived in Goshen which was part of Egypt and not their own real home.

Many years before, a wise Hebrew called Joseph had helped the Egyptians, and Pharaoh, the King of Egypt, had said that Joseph could bring his family to live in Egypt as well. Joseph had eleven brothers. Those brothers had wives and children too. As time went on the family got much bigger. Soon there were so many of them that the Egyptians grew worried. 'Perhaps they will take over our country,' they said.

The new Pharaoh was afraid of the Hebrews so he gave very bad and cruel orders that all new Hebrew baby boys were to be killed. It was just at this time that Moses was born. His mother was brave and wise. She loved him and hid him from Pharaoh's soldiers. When he was too big to be hidden safely at home any longer, she made a floating cradle and hid him in the reeds beside the great River Nile. She asked his big sister, Miriam, to hide there too, and keep watch to see what would happen to baby Moses.

A kind-hearted Egyptian Princess came down to the Nile to bathe. She and her servants found Moses, and the Princess decided to adopt him and bring him up as her own son. Miriam shyly went up to the Princess and said: "Your Majesty, if you need a nurse to look after the baby, I think I can find one for you." The Princess agreed. Miriam ran as fast as she could and fetched her mother, who was then given the job she wanted more than anything in the world: nurse to her own son. Although Moses grew up as a rich young Egyptian Prince, his real mother must have told him all about his own people, the Hebrews, and how they were being badly treated by Pharaoh and the Egyptians. Years later, when Moses had grown up, God used him to free the Hebrews from their slavery and lead them to the land which He had promised them.

"What's that basket I can see,
Floating there beneath the tree?"
"Highness, it's a baby boy:
See, he smiles at you with joy!"

"Highness, what is to be done?"
"I'll adopt him as my son,
But I'll need a nurse's aid . . .
Come here, child, don't be afraid!"

Miriam came and curtsied low:
"Highness, there's a nurse I know."
"Go and fetch her, straight away.
Tell her she must start today!"

To her mother swift she ran,
Told her the Princess's plan.
Mother's heart was filled with joy:
Reunited with her boy.

Brave young Miriam watched so well;
Ran with speed her news to tell.
Help us, Lord, like her to be:
Always watching faithfully.

## PRAYER

Dear Lord Jesus, we know that You love and care for us more than we can ever understand. Help us to do our duty faithfully and well like Miriam did when she watched over her baby brother, Moses. Teach us to take extra care of the very young and the very old who need us most. We ask it in Your Name. Amen.

# SAMUEL LISTENS TO GOD

Many years ago, a woman named Hannah longed to have a son. Her husband, Elkanah, was a good man, who loved her and did his best to help her not to be sad about not having a baby. But Hannah was still very unhappy. She went with Elkanah to the Holy Place at Shiloh, where Eli was the Priest. There she prayed that God would give her a son. Eli talked to her and told her that God would answer her prayer.

Soon afterwards she had a baby boy and called him Samuel. When he was old enough she took him to the Holy Place at Shiloh to be trained as a Priest to help Eli.

One night, when Samuel was asleep in the Holy Place, he heard a voice calling his name. Thinking it was Eli wanting help or needing something fetched, Samuel ran through to the place where the old Priest slept and said: "Here I am. You just called me."

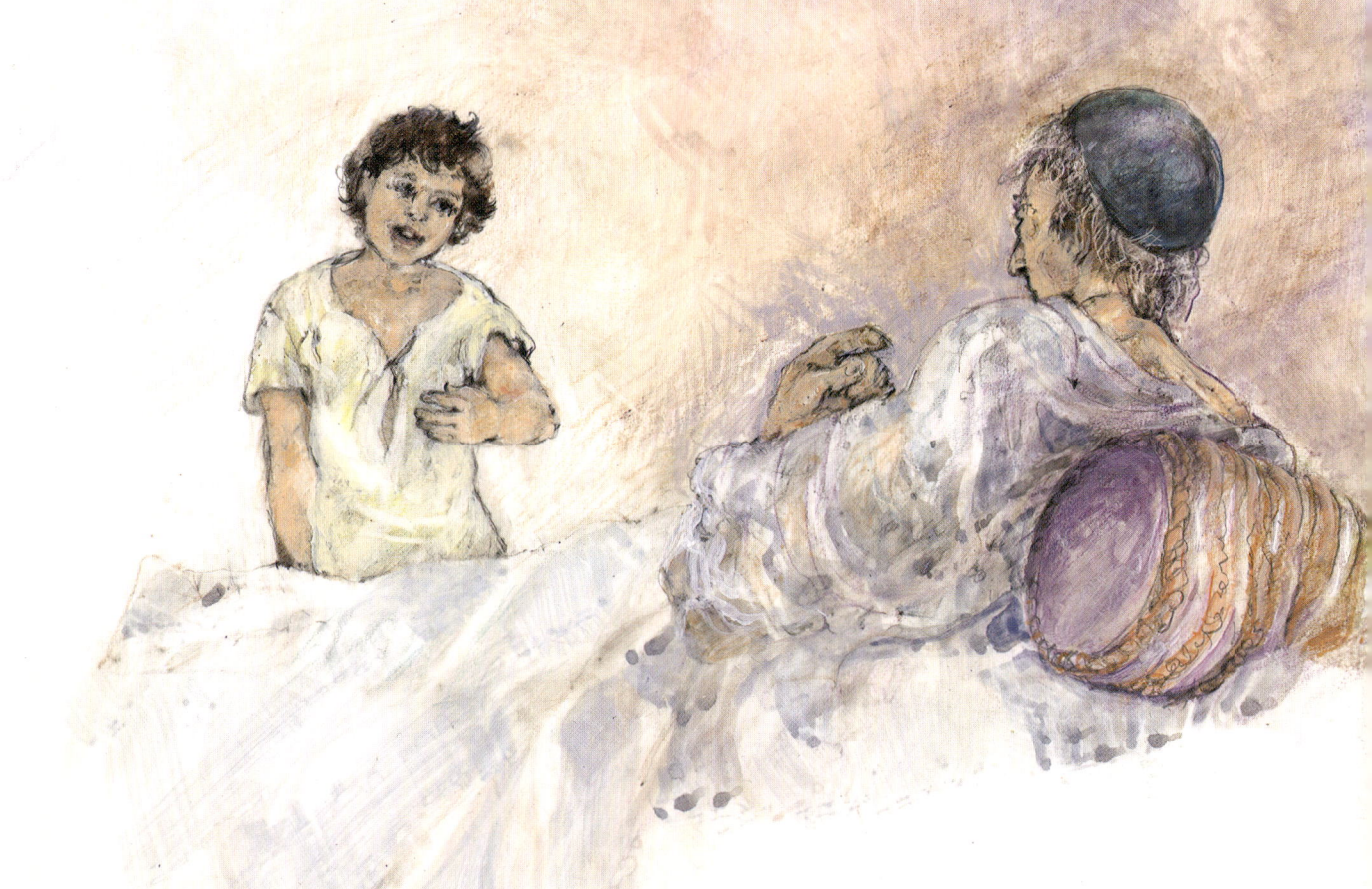

Eli looked at his young friend in surprise. "I didn't call you, my son," he said, sounding rather puzzled. "Go back to sleep." Samuel did as Eli said, but he soon heard the voice again, and ran back to Eli.

"You did call me this time," he said. "I'm sure you did." Once again Eli said that he hadn't called. When it happened a third time, Eli realised that God was speaking to the boy.

"Next time you hear the voice," said the old Priest, "you must answer 'Speak, Lord, for Your servant is listening'" Samuel did what he was told, and God gave him an important message called a prophecy. Samuel grew up to become a great and holy prophet and a leader of his nation because he had the gift of listening to God.

## POEM

Samuel was sleeping soundly
Where God's Sacred Ark was stored
When a Voice came through the stillness
With a message from the Lord.

Samuel thought his master, Eli,
Had been calling from nearby.
Eli said, "I did not call you.
Rest again as down you lie."

Once again there came God's message
Through the silence of the shrine.
Eli told his young assistant
That the message was divine.

"Speak, Lord, for thy servant heareth."
Samuel answered God's command;
Grew to be a mighty prophet,
Judge and leader of the land.

## PRAYER

Loving Heavenly Father, speak to us as you spoke to the Prophet Samuel long ago, and give us the grace to hear Your Voice. Make us loving, kind, gentle and good to others, and show us how to help all those who are in need. We ask it for Jesus' sake. Amen.

# DAVID, THE BRAVE SHEPHERD BOY

A long, hard war was being fought between the Hebrews and the Philistines. The Philistines had a champion called Goliath, who was much bigger than ordinary men. He was so tall that he couldn't have walked through a normal doorway without stooping down. The top of his head would have been very close to the ceiling of most rooms. He was broad and strong as well as tall, and he was the champion of the whole Philistine army. He had been a soldier for many years.

He strode proudly up and down in the space between the two armies. "Send your champion to fight with me!" he shouted to the Hebrews, but no-one wanted to go and fight against him because he was so big.

David was a young shepherd boy, but he was very brave and strong for his age. He had already killed a lion and a bear to save his sheep, and he was not afraid of Goliath.

"I will fight the giant," he said to Saul, the King of the Hebrews, "and I know that God will help me."

Goliath had armour on. He carried a huge spear; and a long, sharp sword hung from his belt. David had no sword, no spear and no armour. He chose five smooth stones from the brook because they were just right for his sling. Hebrew shepherds were very good at using slings. A sling had two cords which you held in your hand, and there was a pouch, like a little leather cup, in the middle. This was made to hold the stone. First you had to spin the sling around your head; then you let go of the end of *one* cord so that the stone would fly out fast and go the way you wanted it to. It took many hours of practice to do it well. David's first stone hit Goliath in the middle of the forehead: he fell heavily to the ground. David ran to him quickly and used Goliath's own sword to cut off the giant's head. When they saw that their champion was dead the other Philistines ran away. With God's help, David had won the battle for the Hebrews.

## POEM

Goliath was a man of war:
The biggest giant you ever saw!
But he was full of boastful pride:
"Who dares to fight with me?" he cried.

David was just a shepherd boy,
But God was David's strength and joy:
"I'll fight Goliath," David said,
And very soon the giant lay dead.

God is the Lord of little things,
Of lambs, and shepherd boys with slings.
When giant problems block our way
Let's do what David did ... *and pray.*

## PRAYER

God of David, we praise and thank You because You love and look after us as You loved and looked after him. Sometimes we have very big problems to overcome. Help us to win life's battles just as You helped David to beat Goliath. Help us to fight the giants of selfishness, greed, fear and laziness, who try to spoil our lives. Put into our hands the sling of honesty, and the five stones of truth, courage, wisdom, determination and hope. We ask it for the sake of Jesus Christ, our Lord. Amen.

# THE BOY WITH THE ARROWS

David, the shepherd boy who killed Goliath, grew up to be a strong and brave soldier. Saul was still King of Israel at this time, and he had a son called Jonathan. Jonathan was David's best friend, and David was Jonathan's best friend. Sadly, King Saul was jealous of David. More than once Saul tried to kill David. It all depended upon what sort of mood Saul was in. If he was all right, then it was safe for David to be in the palace. If Saul was in a bad and angry mood it was dangerous for David.

Jonathan arranged a secret code with David. Jonathan was to pretend that he was going out to do some target practice with his bow and arrows. He had a young servant boy with him. This boy's job was to fetch the arrows after Jonathan had finished shooting.

David was to hide in the bushes and listen. If Jonathan shouted to the boy, "Come this way, the arrows are nearer to me," it meant that Saul was in a good mood so it was safe for David to come back to the palace.

If Jonathan shouted, "The arrows are beyond you, go farther away," it meant that Saul was in a bad mood and David would not be safe in the palace. It was the second message that Jonathan gave, so David knew he would have to leave. He and Jonathan were both very sorry about that because they were such good friends and liked to be together.

The boy who fetched the arrows had no idea about their secret code. He just got on with his job and did as he was told.

Sometimes we don't understand *why* certain things have to be done, but if we trust God, like the boy trusted Jonathan, and follow God's rules, things will work out well, and we shall be playing our part in God's great plan, just as that boy played an important part in the plan that saved the life of David, who would one day become Israel's greatest King.

*POEM*

Young Jonathan was David's friend;
From Saul he sought his life to save;
A code in falling arrows hid
To shield his comrade from the grave.

The boy who looked for fallen shafts
Had no idea of what they meant.
He only went where he was told
To find the arrows which were spent.

Lord make us faithful like that lad,
That we our simple jobs may do:
Content to do Your Will each day
And leave the Greater Plan to You.

*PRAYER*

God of all wisdom, Lord of all knowledge, teach us to trust You more and more. Help us to follow our simple, daily tasks of doing Your Will and obeying Your Holy Laws. Give us grace to serve and worship You properly, to say our prayers often, and to be kind to other people because You love them too. We ask it for the sake of Jesus Christ, our Lord, Amen.

# THE POOR WIDOW AND HER SON

There had been no rain for a long time. The crops would not grow, and there was a terrible famine. Many people were starving. God told Elijah the prophet to go to Zarephath, and Elijah did what God said.

When he got there he saw a poor widow and her young son. They were gathering wood to make a small cooking fire, but they had only enough flour and cooking oil left to make two small cakes. They were afraid that after those little cakes had been eaten they would slowly die of hunger.

Elijah said, "Make me a small cake first." Although they had scarcely any food, and were so hungry themselves, the widow and her son made a cake for Elijah. Her faith and her kindness to Elijah were greatly rewarded. A wonderful miracle happened: from that day onwards there was *always* just enough oil in the cruse and just enough flour in the barrel to feed them every day until the famine was over. God's power provided for the widow, her son and the holy prophet.

*POEM*

The widow and her son
Had used all their supply:
Only enough for one last meal —
Then sit and wait to die.

The mighty prophet came,
Filled with God's strength and power.
"Make first for me a little cake
From your last oil and flour."

Although the hunger filled
Their bodies like a pain,
They carried out the prophet's word:
The flour came back again!

Their oil did not run dry
Nor was the flour spent:
So day by day she made their food.
They ate and were content.

*PRAYER*

Most loving and generous heavenly Father, helper of the poor and helpless, feeder of the hungry, Your power and love provide for us. We do not always remember to thank You for Your gifts. Please forgive us when we forget, and help us to be grateful. Teach us to be generous to others as You are generous to us. Give us the faith and courage of Elijah, the poor widow and her son. Help us through all our troubles as You helped them through that famine long ago. We ask it for the sake of Your Son, Jesus Christ our Lord. Amen.

# THE GIRL WHO HELPED CAPTAIN NAAMAN

The mighty prophet Elijah who saved the widow and her son was followed by another powerful prophet with a name that was *almost* the same as his. This second prophet was called Elisha.

During Elisha's time there lived a great and famous soldier, a leader of the Syrian army. This soldier's name was Naaman. (It is a good name, and it means "pleasant".) He lived up to his name because he was a good and pleasant man as well as a brave, rich and powerful one. He was also kind to his servants: in fact, he was more like a father to them than a master. Because he was so kind to them, they liked him and worked hard for him.

But Naaman had a serious problem: he had a very bad disease called leprosy and in those days nobody knew how to cure it.

Among his servants was a little Jewish girl. One day she said to Naaman's wife, "I wish we all lived in Israel, because there is a great prophet there called Elisha. With God's power, he can cure leprosy. I am sure he could make my master well."

When Naaman heard the news he hurried to Israel to find Elisha. The prophet told him to wash seven times in the River Jordan. At first Naaman was rather upset by these instructions. He had expected something very different from Elisha. He had hoped that the prophet would have put his hands on him and prayed aloud to God for his healing.

"We have rivers in Syria which are better than the Jordan!" said Naaman angrily. Once again, it was the servants who liked him so much who helped him get over his anger and see sense.

"If the prophet had told you to do something hard, you would have done it," they said. "Surely it would be wise to do this simple thing?"

Naaman saw the truth of what his servants were saying.

"You're right!" he said. He did exactly what Elisha had told him and his leprosy was healed at once. He thanked God with all his heart and went home very happy. We can be sure that he gave the little Jewish girl a lovely present when he got home. She might even have been with him on the journey to see Elisha.

### POEM

The Syrian Captain Naaman,
Was strong in heart and mind,
Yet he was also fatherly,
And gentle, good and kind.

Their little Hebrew servant girl
To Naaman's wife had said:
"I wish you and my master lived
In Israel instead!"

"There dwells a prophet great and strong
Who can God's truth reveal,
And if my master went to him
His leprosy would heal."

These words soon reached the captain's ear.
To Israel he rode;
And there — by God's almighty power —
His healing was bestowed.

Oh, may we be like that young maid!
To spread such truth abroad,
Which healing brings to those in need
And glory to the Lord.

PRAYER    Lord of all health and healing, please help and heal all sick people today as you helped Naaman, the Syrian captain, long ago. Help us to tell others about good and important things, like that little Hebrew servant girl told Naaman's wife about Elisha, Your prophet. We ask it for the sake of Jesus Christ, our Lord. Amen.

# JESUS AS A BOY GOES TO THE TEMPLE

When Jesus was twelve years old he was taken to the Temple at Jerusalem to become a 'Son of the Law'. This still happens for Jewish boys today, and is called in Hebrew a Bar-Mitzvah. One very important part of the service is the point where the boy has to read aloud from one of the sacred scrolls of the Law.

Even though He was still very young, Jesus was full of wisdom and holy power, and the teachers of the Law (who were called Rabbis in Hebrew) were amazed at how much He knew. Jesus Himself was very interested in His Father's Law, and was happy to talk to the Rabbis about it. When the time came for Mary and Joseph to go back to their home in Nazareth, Jesus was still listening to the wise old Rabbis and asking them deep questions. Joseph and Mary thought that Jesus had gone on ahead of them with some friends of His own age, or with some other members of their family. When they found out that He was missing they were very worried and hurried back to Jerusalem to look for Him.

Mary and Joseph looked everywhere for Jesus. At last they went back to the Temple: and there He was — still talking to the Rabbis.

Mary and Joseph told Him how worried they had been. "We were very sad," they told Him. "We didn't know where You were, and we were afraid that something terrible had happened to You."

"You shouldn't have worried," said Jesus gently. "Didn't you know that I would be in my Father's House doing my Father's work?" In this quiet and loving way Jesus reminded Mary and Joseph that He was really God's Son and that He had a very special job to do for His Father while He was on earth with us.

Mary and Joseph loved Jesus very much, and were so glad to find that He was safe. They told Him how pleased they were that they had found Him, then they all set off for Nazareth, happy to be together.

*POEM*

Mary and Joseph took our Lord
When He was twelve years old
Into the sacred Temple Court
Where Holy Truth was told.

As they went back to Nazareth,
Our Lord they could not find.
"We must return at once," they said.
"Jesus is left behind!"

They looked for Jesus everywhere:
Then in the Temple Court
Among the Rabbis old and wise
They found the One they sought.

"Why was it that you looked for Me?"
The Son of God replied.
"Did you not know that I would be
My Father's House inside?"

*PRAYER*   Blessed Lord Jesus, You knew how important it was to go to Your Father's House to pray and to talk about His Law even while You were still a boy. Teach us to follow Your example, and to love being in God's House. Teach us to love, honour and respect our parents, as You loved, honoured and respected Mary and Joseph while You were growing up in Nazareth. We ask it for Your Name's sake. Amen.

# THE BOY WHO GAVE JESUS HIS BREAD AND FISH

A huge crowd followed Jesus because of the wonderful things He did and the wonderful things He said. Whenever He used God's power to heal people who were ill, more and more people came out to see what was happening. Many of them had come a long way, and they had brought nothing to eat. Jesus asked the disciples to see whether there was any food to be found to give to the people.

Andrew, who was Simon Peter's brother, brought to Jesus a boy who had five barley loaves and two fishes, which he had brought for his own meal. Very willingly the boy gave this food to Jesus.

Our Lord then told the disciples to ask the people to sit down. Then He gave thanks to God for the loaves and fish, and broke them up to share among all those *thousands* of people There was more than enough for everyone. At the end of the meal, Jesus told the disciples to gather up the pieces that were left over. Those pieces filled twelve baskets. All the people who shared in that feast were amazed. They realised that Jesus was Someone very, very special.

## POEM

A lad with two fishes and five loaves of bread,
Once gave them to Jesus, and thousands were fed.
That boy's simple faith in the power of the Lord
Brought blessings from Heaven where all gifts are stored.

Our Lord took those gifts in His strong, loving hands;
Gave thanks to His Father, the Lord of all lands;
Then gently He broke up the bread and the fish:
The people enjoyed all the food they could wish.

Lord, help us to be like that lad who was there.
Please make us more loving and eager to share.
The smallest of gifts which we offer to You
Is blessed and increased by what God's power can do.

## PRAYER

Dear Lord Jesus, You are always able to take our smallest gifts and make them useful to You and to others. Help us to be like the boy who gave You his loaves and fish. Show us ways of serving You and our brothers and sisters. We know that God our Father wants us to be kind, generous and helpful to one another. Take away our selfishness, and help us to think of others. Take away our greed, and make us generous to the poor and helpless. Our ordinary, daily lives are like that boy's plain bread and fish: please take them as our gift and make them into something good, useful and beautiful for God and the people around us. We ask it for Your Name's sake. Amen.

# JESUS BLESSES THE CHILDREN

As our Lord's work went on, more and more people heard about His teachings, His miracles and His healings. Many of the mothers in the place where He was working wanted Him to bless their children. All good mothers want what is best for their sons and daughters, and these mothers knew that there was nothing better in all the world than a blessing from Jesus.

His disciples, however, knew that their Master was very tired from long hours of preaching, teaching and healing. They were trying to save Jesus from any extra work until He had had some rest. That was why they told the mothers to take their children away and not bother Jesus.

Our Lord heard what was going on. He called the mothers and their children to Him to be blessed.

"You must not send them away," he told His disciples. "Always let the little children come to me; our Heavenly Father loves them very much and wants them to share His Kingdom."

## POEM

The little ones to Jesus came
All to be blessed that day.
"He's resting," the disciples said,
"So you must go away!"

The children and their mothers felt
Unhappy then, and sad.
But Jesus woke and smiled at them;
And then they all felt glad.

"Come unto Me, My little ones,"
Their Saviour gently said.
He blessed each tiny boy and girl:
Strong hands on each small head.

To His disciples then He spoke:
"God loves these children well —
Encourage them to come to Me;
My love for them please tell."

## PRAYER

Dear Lord Jesus, we love to hear how You welcomed and blessed children like us. We know that when You told the disciples to make the children welcome, You meant that welcome to be for all children in every land and for all time. We know that You welcome us in our country today, just as You welcomed those children and their mothers in the Holy Land long ago.

Please teach us to welcome and bless others as You welcomed and blessed them. Help us to understand that all the other boys and girls we meet, in our homes, while we are playing, or in our schools, are very dear to You. Help us all to love and be kind to one another because we know that You love us all, and You want us to make one another happy.

We ask it for Your name's sake.

Amen.

# SAINT PAUL IS SAVED BY HIS YOUNG NEPHEW

Saint Paul was in great danger because some people who wanted to stop him preaching about Jesus had made a plot to kill him. His sister's young son was a brave, wise and loyal boy, who overheard this plot against his uncle. He told Saint Paul and the Roman Captain what he had just heard, and this very important news saved his uncle's life.

*POEM*

> News of plotting just begun
> Carried to Paul's sister's son.
> He with loyal courage true
> Told his uncle what he knew.
>
> That young nephew, wise and brave,
> Did his famous uncle save.
> Let us, Lord, like that lad be:
> Helping those who toil for Thee.

*PRAYER*

Loving Heavenly Father, help us to be like Paul's nephew. Make us as brave, loyal, alert and thoughtful as he was. Make us aware of what's happening in Your world, and teach us to use that knowledge to play our small part to help good men and women in their fight against evil. We ask it for the sake of Jesus Christ, Your Son, our Lord. Amen.